FISH LOVE

Advance Praise

"Bryanna Licciardi's *Fish Love* is full of regret—in the best way possible. In these poems, regret becomes a passageway, opening door after door, leading to both knowledge and acceptance of the self, a self that is creative and cruel in turns. These poems explore identity as constructed by geography, genes, and gender: 'I'm still unraveling,' the speaker notes, 'the truth that *belonging* means offering up / pieces of yourself like sacrifice.' It's a strategically unsettling book as it juxtaposes narratives of serial killers alongside memories of difficult grandmothers, of problematic parents, of the ongoing frustration with 'the realization / that my dissatisfaction was not / with people, but with / their predictability.' *Fish Love* is anything but predictable. It evades the hook as it limns the space between desire and destruction, between loving and changing the self, between regret and slippery, fishy relief."
—Amie Whittemore, author of *Glass Harvest*

"Ah, love! In Bryanna Licciardi's hands, the slippery fish makes virgins into sex addicts and women into desserts because they, too, are 'served last.' To swim in this school is to reason with babies one never plans to have and learn that 'freedom is a sword / with too many edges.' *Fish Love* finds us all outmatched by the depths, unless we let love off the hook for its fishiness and let it lure us beyond ourselves."
—Amy Wright, author of *Paper Concert*

"In Bryanna Licciardi's piercingly observant collection, profound longing and nostalgia introduce us to a speaker aware and prescient of the body, political and sensual, in all its complexities. The body is one, the body is multiple, Licciardi reminds us, as she writes simultaneously toward and away from childhood memory. She also reminds us that originality

has to do with what is timeless turned sideways: 'After months of thinking otherwise, / I am concluding less and less.' Formally inventive, syntactically animate, *Fish Love* is sinister and funny, egoless and immaculate, and convinces us how '*belonging* means offering up / pieces of yourself like sacrifice.'"
—Gary McDowell, author of *Aflame*

FISH LOVE

poems

BRYANNA LICCIARDI

Alternating Current Press
Boulder, Colorado

Copyright © 2024 Bryanna Licciardi
All rights reserved

Published by Alternating Current Press
Boulder, Colorado 80302
altcurrentpress.com
All rights reserved

Library of Congress Control Number: 2024933406
ISBN-13 (paperback): 978-1-946580-50-4
ISBN-10 (paperback): 1-946580-50-3
ISBN-13 (hardcover): 978-1-946580-51-1
ISBN-13 (ebook): 978-1-946580-52-8

Interior and cover design: Leah Angstman
Author photo: Kelly Chapman Photography © 2022, 2024

The following is a work of fiction created by the author. All names, individuals, places, items, brands, events, characters, &c., are the product of the author's imagination, are used fictitiously, or are entirely coincidental.

No part of this publication may be reproduced, stored in a retrieval system, or transmitted, in any form or by any means, electronic, mechanical, photocopied, recorded, or otherwise, without the prior permission of Alternating Current Press, except for the quotation of brief passages used inside of an article, criticism, or review.

Printed in the United States of America

10 9 8 7 6 5 4 3 2 1

Table of Contents

i. don't tell me you love the fish

Double Dream 17
Assigned Buddies 18
They Called Him Bear 20
Someone Sets Me Up with Charles Manson 21
Hopalong Cassidy Was Grandmother's Hero 22
Catch 23

ii. you love yourself

Their Destroyed Mouths 27
Think about Jellybeans as You Die 28
Seasonal 29
Temple Building 31
I'm 13 & Mom Convinces Me Period Blood Is Sacred 32
Reimagining My Birth as Zeus & Athena 34
Dealing 35

iii. tastes good

Dear Stephen King 41
Lies I Told My Baby Brother 43
Eating Mercy 44
Interview with Mercy 46
Twenty-Seven-Year-Old Virgin Sex Addict 47
Tidal Waves 48

iv. out of water

Trying to Reason with the Baby I Never Plan to Have 53
Losing Weight 55
Thoughts I Don't Share While
 Out to Dinner with a New Guy 57
Fragments of a False Elegy 59
When the Bank Says My Account Was Drained 61
A Millennial's Unfinished Odes to Her Many Terrible Jobs 63
20th Anniversary 65

v. killed it, boiled it

H. H. Holmes Steals a Cadaver for Our Date 69
A Guilt Trap Has Many Teeth 70
Reconciling 72
Mantras of an Anxious Child 74
My Brother Tells Us about Catching Teenagers
 Stealing Shoes at the Department Store 75
Dream Where My Teeth Fall Out 76

vi. most of love, is fish love

Ax 81
Found on or Near Jack Parsons' Body, Post-Blast 82
Beasts 84
If I Moved to Truth or Consequences 85
What I Meant When I Said Love 87
Bless the Chocolate with Sprinkles 88
Body Worship Takes Work 90
Fish Love 92

To my love,
for showing it back.

He said, "Don't tell me you love the fish. You love yourself. And because the fish tastes good to you, you took it out of the water and killed it and boiled it." So much of what is love, is fish love.

—Rabbi Dr. Abraham Twerski

i.
don't tell me you love the fish

Double Dream

Now that you're gone
the night craves us.
I listen as it stirs and
settles, stirs and unsettles.
You might have told me
the house is shifting,
that my Stephen King
obsession has left me
too many monsters,
but now, with the lights off,
everything feels heavy—
my arms, our bed, sheets,
even an open window
starts to fall, as if the night
has kidnapped our days,
stuffed them into
a thousand dark suitcases,
and now regrets
all this weight.

Assigned Buddies

The teacher says these girls are good for me
because my twang is a target, and at first,
I agree. Even after they push lunch trays
at me to put away, tell me not to speak without
permission, call me redneck that time I say *y'all*.

It's too cold here to feel like myself.
My parents have bought us foreign clothes
—snow pants, thermal underwear.
Not until the sun comes do I realize how much
I've missed my own clothes. Like my overalls.
I love how they don't slip down my scrawny hips
the way jeans do. Today I'm strutting

the hallways, feeling freely myself.
Kids pass, pointing and belly laughs that
I don't understand. On the bus, my buddies say
only hicks wear overalls. I'm an embarrassment.
I'd like to tell you I made them lick dirt,

but it's third grade, and I'm still unraveling
the truth that *belonging* means offering up
pieces of yourself like sacrifice.
I'm the new girl who talks funny,
who doesn't know cursive or the times table,
who needs the teacher's help
to put on her snow pants.

At home, I rip off the overalls,
throw them in the trash bin outside, but
that's not enough distance between us,
so I grab a can of Pearly Pink paint
left over from my new room,
and pour it over the denim like frosting.
I wait then, for relief, or regret
—whichever comes first.

They Called Him Bear

Not because his arms looked like
two watermelons devoured by cobras,

or the mass of fur poking through his shirt.
Not because his laugh shook the car.

Not because his hands were clawing beneath my straps,
or because his smile was all sharp and predator.

Not because he parked us by the woods
after I'd fallen asleep.

Not because his car became a cave.
Not because his hunger.

They called him Bear because
he was their protector.

A loving father, husband,
and of all people there that night, at that party,

with him, they said,
I would be safe.

Someone Sets Me Up with Charles Manson

Serial killer charged with inciting murder, though never found guilty of committing a murder himself.

But I get there to find Charles has sent two guys in his place. They eat like wolves and want me to pay because Charles told them I would, and I do. I ask if he'll show up later, and they tell me, *Maybe, but he's Manson, Son of Men—so it's hard to say.* The taller guy puts his hand on my knee and winks. The other one, gnashing meat through his teeth when he smiles, has a Southern accent and asks me to call him Cowboy. Eventually I make an excuse to leave, can't recall why I even showed, but they follow me into my car and fling off their shoes. I roll down the windows because it smells so bad. *Where can I drop you off?* I say. *What's the rush?* they want to know. Cowboy asks if I'd like to see their ranch, learn about the coming war, possibly bang The Man himself. I've finally discovered my sanity, so I tell them, *When pigs fly*, and the tall one says, *Oh, they may not fly, but boy, do we make them run.*

Hopalong Cassidy Was Grandmother's Hero

After each episode, I imagine young her
blazing a rusted bike through the streets,
desperately in search of that Wild West.

In dreams, I'm there, too,
watching her posed small against
a black-and-white screen.

I want to warn her, *Don't turn around!*
I want to promise that life's better
if you know to look this way.

But Hopalong always gets booted for Technicolor.
And my grandmother's back stays turned
to what's coming: the rapturing static.

Catch

> *(noun): the point in a swimmer's stroke when their hand grabs at the water in front of them and applies pressure to move the body forward*

Distant cheers are seeping through,
but beneath the water, I'm mad:
forced between hydrogen and oxygen,
chlorine burning my throat despite

the protections of this mask, despite
bottoms that cut into my hips.
Both are making it harder to breathe.
A chant begins, something about the finish line,

and I glance up, making out your shape
through the ripples, stooped over the pool,
waiting to help me up from my victory lap.
I keep pushing under and through.

When I picture our wet-hugged moment,
I'm reminded of another, at our friend's party
where I saw you, but never told you,
swaying to music among stacks of people,
your stomach touching hers like I thought only for me,

and I stop: legs unpumping, arms uncatching.
I finally hear my lungs filling with weight,
saying I was never safe down here,
and everyone is cheering.

ii.
you love yourself

Their Destroyed Mouths

inspired by the work of Rosario Castellanos

wanted to climb
inside my mouth

tongues that could have
felt luxurious

instead split me
into tiny rooms

once they pillaged my body
so that no one would want me

once I felt ruined
and they called it love

it's sweetly scented words
shoveled into our mouths

that make this destruction
so stunning

Think about Jellybeans as You Die

Let your tongue taste
the waxy sweet without fear.

Think of the way each candy will burst
between your teeth with lovely savagery.

Remember learning how to swim,
to pick your battles, mind your tongue,

that first slice of cake, that last time
you were told your body doesn't belong to you.

Remember learning that women, like dessert,
are served last. People may tell you

to avoid mistaking violence for passion,
but in those final moments,

their falsely fruited smell will exhilarate you.
Let the sweet bring you home—

a beautiful, dead thing.

Seasonal

We're in the kitchen doing dishes when
Mom tells me I'm part Hungarian.
She gives me a word. *Cigán*.
It means Gypsy, she says,
handing over a bowl to dry.
I say it, too, and fall in love with
the way it rolls over my tongue,
warm like cinnamon.
I ask if she knows any Gypsies.
She tips a plate back and forth
across the faucet's stream.

My grandfather grows peaches in his yard,
which Mom calls a jungle. His house, too,
with newspaper stacks tall as trees,
batteries and journals in piles so wide
only he knows how to swoop
through each corridor.
He chose to stop speaking for 20 years.
Mom says it never made a difference to her—
silence was just another distance between them.
If he remembered, he'd call
on her birthday and whistle a song.

At the table, I pour myself a glass of milk.
Mom's back is to me as she wipes the counter.
I whisper it some more, *Cigán. Cigán.* She half turns
to me and smiles. I ask what Gypsies do, though
I'm already picturing myself twirling earthy hips
in dark, exotic woods. *They live by the season,*
she says. Her back again.
A part of me hears how her voice wavers, but
I'm too young, or too far into fantasy.
This time I mouth the word silently,
savoring the way my throat
vibrates the last vowel.

Temple Building

In seventh grade, I determine God is addiction,
but don't tell my parents. They worry as it is.
This is the year Dad fences together a garden.
I try to revel in it with him, but, alone,
the dirt on my hands is terrifying.

When his roses bloom, fragile and pathetic,
how faithfully he still tends them.
I pray, or try to, as he cuts through soil.
My job is to find weeds he says will choke our flowers.
Sometimes I'm afraid I'll miss one, just one,

and our hard work will die,
because of that weed, because of me.
Within the month, Dad finds rabbits in our yard.
He takes me to the garden center to buy bags of
dried blood, a trick passed down from his mother.

We scatter the powder. I ask if the blood is real.
He looks toward something beyond our house
when he answers, *They hate the smell.*
Smells like death. I want to ask what's wrong with death,
but instead leave to wash it from my hands.

I'm 13 & Mom Convinces Me Period Blood Is Sacred

She says first blood
cures many things.
She says this to my acne,
not me. We're eating
dinner, and I'm pushing
around mashed potatoes
telling her that she's crazy.
Lost it. She says beauty
beats crazy, any day.
I try to touch my face, but
she pushes my hand away,
and by the time I go to bed,
even the pillow feels like
an attack against my skin.

Then it happens.
I'm standing there,
door locked, pants heavy on my feet,
holy brightness of red
between my legs both
cruel and mesmerizing.

I lean against the sink,
eyes on this new me.
Eyes to forehead, cheeks,
to hands that have started without me—
these fingers smearing battle paint
across my face.

Now I hold my breath.
Now I wait for this blessing to break.
Now I wait for the breaking sound.

Reimagining My Birth as Zeus & Athena

Mother is standing by, apron-tied,
some of her curls already frizzing
despite layers of mousse.

This morning, it's way too hot.
I'm suffocating, frantic to get out.
Push against his ribs. Ignore

the swells and splinters.
My palms sticky with acid.
A taste in my mouth
like dirty pennies.

I'm gagging now, clawing,
desperate to rip bone and skin aside
when, finally, exhausted, I emerge.

Mother is stirring tea at the table.
There's plenty for both of us,
she says and pours another cup.

Isn't it too hot for tea? I say,
but sit anyway. We pay no mind
to Father's body, now useless
and rancid on the floor.

Dealing

Her aggression has spread to the doctors
who now refuse to speak to her directly,
for fear of those heavy words she swings.
It's been weeks since you found out,
but you haven't called. Haven't written. Instead,
you find an old photo on your computer and email it.
You consider this a nice gesture, but then remember
she doesn't check her email.

Your mom, aunts, brother, really everyone, says how
terrible she's taking it, how unbearable
she's become. You almost buy a plane ticket,
but tell yourself work's too busy.
A visit will only make things worse.
Attention is like chemo with Grandma—she hates it,
needs it, craves it, festers in it. She's knotted now more
than ever in her abnormal cell growth
and conviction that no one loves her.

The longer you don't call, the more guilt invades
your brain. You remember that time she accused you of
being just like your father. Their feud is famous.
Everyone says it's because they're too much alike,
so you know she meant it to be cruel.

～

When you learn cancer can be caused by old cells
refusing to die, it reminds you of that ride to the airport
on her last visit. She wouldn't let you cry, because
a lady should be above such emotional frivolities.
You recall her thin lips crisscrossing into
a thousand lines, then the memory metastasizes into
that pastel pink lipstick she wore every day,
how its shiny gold case glittered in the light.

～

You tell yourself, *Today I'll call*. And the next day,
and the next, and the next, make another reminder,
another promise, knowing it will be
something you'll regret, frozen in this dance
between what is and what you refuse it to be.
Really, isn't everyone a mass of cells,
changing every day? And isn't there always
more time?

iii.
tastes good

Dear Stephen King

You are a vile
and beautiful man.

    Thank you.

For burrowing
into my nightmares,
for bonding me
to the dark,
depraved,
devious spaces
of my brain.

Thanks for
the heroes you denigrated,
the humanity you offered freaks,
the realization
that my dissatisfaction was not
with people, but with
their predictability.

You, who said my monsters
had wisdom to share,
who showed me
that some words feel
too sharp to come out,
that those words are
most necessary—

this is to say
—King of Horror,
prolific prince,
sinister savior
—thanks for offering
my wickedness
such purpose.

Lies I Told
My Baby Brother

With the realtor and our parents in the other room,
that the house was haunted.
I pointed to ghosts outside the window
pushing blades of grass around the lawn.
You said it was the wind. *Dead people*, I insisted.
You couldn't be consoled, and we left
that prospective house in a hurry.

That your real sister was a witch who,
broom tucked under her skirt,
was on her way to you now,
determined to discover how delectable
her little brother would taste.

When you had a cold, that snot was really
memories dripping from your brain,
that blowing your nose meant
losing something you loved.
I called it creative. Mom called it cruel,
probably because of the way you ran around,
hands outstretched as if suddenly blind,
calling out, *Who am I? Who are you?*
And it was funny, until you grabbed at me, crying,
and said you never wanted to forget my face.

Eating Mercy

In 1892, the corpse of teenager Mercy Brown was exhumed and eaten. The town decided a mysterious illness (now known to be tuberculosis) was a symptom of Mercy's wicked curse, and in their desperation, they hoped the mutilation and consumption of her body would save them.

watch them prove me   Death

watch this body burn   watch them pluck

     my organs like fruit

smelling skin & smoke   watch my body

     shrink to cinders

watch them drink   my ashes watch

     the cup he pours of me

his sickness raging   even as he drinks

     watch him choke

watch them need me both wicked & cure

     watch them destroy

watch them   pat one another's backs,

their own bodies   growing tall

    like heroes—

Interview with Mercy

Mercy's grave has since become a darkly beloved tourist attraction.

They fed you to your brother to save his life. Did you ever hope for regret?
> *I am a stain*
> *there is not enough of me to kill*

What about you makes them afraid?
> *they called me Demon*
> *and so I became one*

After all these years, people continue to visit, leaving you gifts, letters. What do they want from you now?
> *they want me to let them go*

What is it like to watch people beg your forgiveness?
> *my death*
> *over and over*
> *passed between their hands*

Why do they hide behind your grave at night?
> *it's a game, you see*
> *whoever finds me*
> *gets to keep me*

Twenty-Seven-Year-Old Virgin Sex Addict

    I think about having it and not—
    piecing apart my body,

and his, and what I'm told of love,

        watching everyone's eyes on me,
        aroused by the thought

they know something I don't.

        My sex has a spine.
        It is empty and aching.

Picture my mouth

        cold and wet in his ear,
        daring him to give this to me.

Tidal Waves

When we are alone,
        he says we should sleep together.
His stale, minty words crush
me into this floor that is
        spreading like waves from my

shoulders, and
        I'm pulled to the time
my brother and I, bored, pitched a chair
into the pool, just to watch something sink.
        A man's love has always felt

like drowning. This night,
        his eyes teach me how
to fear my body,
hands that speak
        this is all I'll ever mean.

iv.
out of water

Trying to Reason with the Baby I Never Plan to Have

Know that it takes one thousand days to detox,
and my weekly trip to the winery is unavoidable.
Know that big heads run in my family,
that a baby's head makes up 25 percent of its length,
that Einstein's brain was 15 percent wider than normal
and you would definitely be smarter than Einstein.

Know that Americans are overeaters,
that you would probably be obese because
my cat is obese, and because I eat
when I'm upset and babies upset me.

Know that aliens like to abduct babies at night,
that I sleep with the windows open, that aliens
run in my family, that they say kids
are growing up faster these days,
that girls have faster heartbeats,
boys blink less, that unlike other humans,
identical twins have the same exact scent,
that babies are born with 100 extra bones,
and I can't decide which one of those facts
freaks me out more.

Know that people live better
without food than sleep,
that babies don't understand the concept
of night and day, that I must go to bed by 8 o'clock
or I'm no good, that high levels of testosterone
make you feel pleasure from inflicting pain,
that testosterone runs in my family.

Know that anger increases people's desire
to possess things, and I can barely share
a bottle of wine, that I've been known to hide it
before company arrives.

Know that having you would eat at least 20 percent
of my salary,
and my figure,
that by not having you,
I can avoid the wage gap,
and though people see this
as proof of lesbianism, or alienism,
I'm okay with that.

Know that it's been scientifically proven
you'd hear my voice in the womb,
and I can't sing worth a damn.
Know that if you died,
hearing is the last sense to go.
That when the heart stops before the brain,
you might have been able to hear me
saying your name.

Losing Weight

Five pounds:
I began ignoring mirrors after
Thoreau appeared one night,
urging me to gnaw my bones.
You'll love it, he said,
lightly touching my neck.
My spine scuttled in his hands.

Ten pounds:
Now my dog leaves the room
when I walk in.
He's hurt. He misses the way
I'd rub his chin
and let him lick the spoon.

Fifteen pounds:
In an infomercial,
God said he'd show me how
to give up perfection
and love myself
for only three easy payments
of $29.95.
I didn't want to believe
my body is a thing.

Thirty pounds:
I saw Moses in my bed.
He parted the sheets, asked
which side I preferred,
so I rolled over and will
continue to do so
until he tells me I'm finished,
or until it's morning.

Fifty pounds:
The world got bigger.
The Buddha said it would,
that it needed to
before he could show me how
to plant the good seeds, how to eat
the good fruit.

Thoughts I Don't Share While Out to Dinner with a New Guy

They say a lady never orders more
than one cocktail,
which is why I carry
a flask in my purse.

It's hard to concentrate.
Your biceps are quite distracting.

I've been told I make intense
eye contact—tell me
what you're thinking!

Mother just texted.
She likes the picture I took
of you ordering the chicken,
thinks we'll make
an adorable Christmas card.

If an octopus and a penguin mated,
what would they call it? An octoguin?

I've grown fond of falling asleep
to the coital sounds
of my upstairs neighbors.

A pengopus?

Gravity is my favorite force,
the way it gives grace to everything
that falls, and I regret
not being perfect.

My bedroom window is bare
because shopping for curtains should be
an act of lovemaking
between two people.

Though you won't love me
the way I need,
I've already let myself
believe you will.

There is a piece of spinach in your teeth.

Fragments of
a False Elegy

inspired by Rosario Castellanos' poem "Falsa Elegía"

Before you are born
you threaten what exists,
being more than real.

I see children as a scientific equation
used to prove ourselves,
love applied in the form of hypothesis.

Make me dinner.
Watch me slurp spaghetti with sauce,
as if you weren't even there,
as if it's the best you've ever had.

I remember the way my parents used
their hands on my back to reassure me.
How the slowness of your fingers
I once mistook for desire.

~~

Watch me paint my fingernails and peel
the dried polish, each piece becoming
a small, curved mask to drop away.

~~

After months of thinking otherwise,
I am concluding less and less.

When the Bank Says My Account Was Drained

by someone from Texas,
when they say my hundreds of hours
worked at three jobs has been
over weeks—$50 here, $20 there—
stolen away, money saved for
my move to graduate school,

when they ask do I know anyone
from that area, I think back to the night
you helped me move into my dorm
because it was my first night away from home,
and you knew I was scared,
also terrible at making new friends,

but especially, I think how by night
we were both starved because I hadn't thought
to bring food for the fridge,
so we drove around this strange town
in search of groceries, ending at a gas station
with no name and expired cans of Vienna sausage,

where I had to decide between spending my change
on Cheetos or toilet paper,
and we laughed so hard stuffing loose paper
from their bathroom in our purses,
knowing this was our first ridiculous act as adults,
how by the time we got back

so much night had gone by
that we crashed into the bed too small for even me
with happy, orange-stained fingertips,
so, now, please tell me—
how do I explain any of this
to the banker on the phone?

And months after I move
when you text *hey you,*
how about a visit soon?
—what in me chose to respond
maybe soon, miss you friend.

A Millennial's Unfinished Odes to Her Many Terrible Jobs

To the man whom,
as you ordered your Happy Meal,
I had a strong desire to kiss
because you smelled like sage,
but didn't because
you had too many kids—

To my boss at the grocery store
who banished me to pushing carts
each time I dropped a jar at the checkout,
which was every shift—

To that time I worked at a gym,
and overheard this sweaty, spandexed woman
tell someone that looking like me
would be her nightmare—

To the gym—

To the dad at the drive-thru
for asking me to go out with
his 12-year-old son
because he'd just won third place
at a skateboard contest
and deserved a hot date—

To the movie theater manager
who dared me to eat an entire box of Twizzlers,
who laughed when I puked,
who fired me two weeks later—

To that same boss who escorted Elise
to her car at night, but not me,
because I looked like
"the kind of girl who doesn't get mugged"—

To the hairdresser at the salon
who offered me a free haircut
while I was sweeping the floor
and afterward complained
about my terrible haircut—

To the 5-year-old girl I caught
in the salon's bathroom,
desperately licking the wall—

To her parents—

20th Anniversary

Dad sneaks me to a flower shop in town.
It's the first time he's ever asked my advice,
so I'm nervous but secretly pleased.

I tell him to buy her yellow roses, because
they smell sweet, and yellow means friendship.
She'd accept being friends, at the very least.

When he gives them to her, I hide on the stairs.
Mom's voice is private, but the meanness of it
makes me run back to my room. Our front door slams

hard enough to shake both stories in the house.
I have the music turned up as loud as it will go
by the time Mom tries to knock.

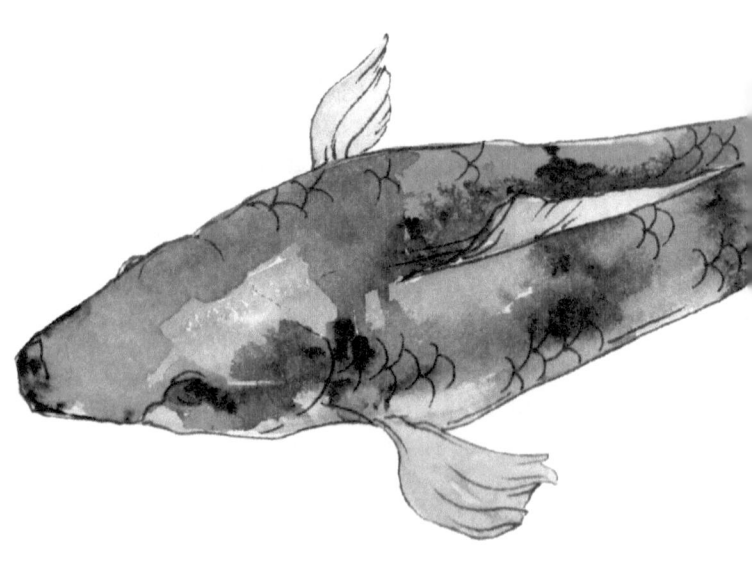

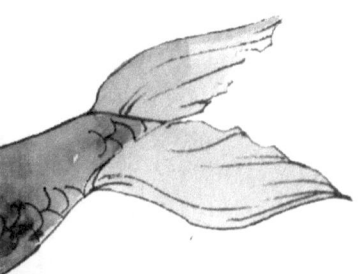

v.
killed it, boiled it

H. H. Holmes Steals a Cadaver for Our Date

Cadaver thievery was a little-known habit of this well-known serial killer.

And I think this might be
the most romantic dinner

ever devoured: slushy caviar,
bubbles in champagne,

lobster, the white linen,
the putrefying body between us,

the way it nuzzles
into my shoulder,

how Holmes tugs it
back straight

so that his own fingertips
can forage my neck.

A Guilt Trap Has Many Teeth

The girl behind me
in math class
liked to roll up her sleeves
and trace her bitten nails
down rousing, red scars,

liked to watch the boys
eye and awe and ask about pain,
liked this to be some kind
of love, or lust;
honestly
I don't think it mattered to her.

They'd lean around me
to get a good look,
and I'd have to wait
until lunch
before I could say out loud
to my friends,
How sad! How disturbed!

and it wasn't until years later
they were exhumed
in a therapist's office—

those strange, hot feelings
of resentment
and envy and shame and
god-awful admiration.

Reconciling

to my father

She liked to teach you
how to make her happy.
To mop the floors shiny,
fold towels with sharp corners.
She saw in you her safe place.
When her husband left,
she drank to fuel anger,
her hurt an honored badge.

You moved 12 states over,
not to get away from her,
though the way she'd changed
couldn't be reconciled.
Sometimes moving can just mean moving on.
After she got sick, your sisters
took her in, but you kept away.
Being sick only made her
more justified in her anger.

Years pass, you hear it's almost over,
and fly back to see her at the hospital.
Her face looks too small,
she's barely there in that bed.
You lean in for one last kiss,
and she grabs your shirt,
lifting herself off the bed,
grates the words, *He did this to me*,
and you see she means it.
You try to remove her grasp,
but instead watch her body
empty like a stairwell.

Mantras of
an Anxious Child

To steady yourself,
you must toss out
dull crayons. Only
sharp edges will do.
Each swipe a spade

through the skin.
To carry yourself,
grip tight the railing.
Count the steps up, down.
Make your hand let go.

To sleep at night,
take to bed your most
trusted doll. Make her
promise she will keep
you anchored, and safe.

Sheets up. Don't forget:
this is how you hold.

My Brother Tells Us about Catching Teenagers Stealing Shoes at the Department Store

The shoes were on sale anyway,
which, he says, makes the teens idiots,
and we start laughing, when my stepdad
Willy interrupts to tell us about the time
he was 13 and his mom had run away, again,
leaving him, again, to take care of his siblings.
Willy says he tried to sneak out
of a store with a can of green beans
when a cashier grabbed him
at the door and dragged him toward
the line of people waiting with carts.
She called him a good-for-shit thief
and dug into his coat. Willy says
the worst part wasn't everyone watching,
or being caught, but the cashier's
eyes when she saw the beans.
The way her face melted, how she
tried to give the can back.
But Willy didn't want it that way
and chucked it to the floor
before he took off running, regretting it
only after getting home—
the giving back the can, not the stealing.
He makes sure to clarify this.

Dream Where My Teeth Fall Out

Tragic holes left in me.
Any way you look at them—
in the head, the ozone,
a beautiful blouse—
holes are never a good thing.

Just before I'm raptured by loss,
a woman approaches with warm hands
as if to say she will love me anyway.
She glows indigo, asks how to help,
but I'm ashamed to open my mouth.
A part of me wants to run away,
to forget the way
our fingers fit together
because I will never again be a good thing.

Another part wants to take her out,
for us to witness together
the wonderful pain of beer cooling
the new nakedness of my gums.
But each time, I wake,
leaving her waiting,
missing my shot at one good thing.

vi.
most of love, is fish love

Ax

I am strung around the room like Christmas lights,

dimmed low blinking. You're walking in

  your sleep again, snacking on communion

like you're a god. Night after night, my skin

lights up for you. This is our game, but it's always

your turn. How about tonight

  I pick the game?

  You be a tree, and I,

the woodsman. One whack to your skull

and look now it's snowing.

  Tonight, let's discover

the many ways I can save your soul.

Found on or Near Jack Parsons' Body, Post-Blast

Jack Parsons, American rocket engineer, inventor, and occult leader, died in 1952 following a home-lab explosion.

singed remnants of his 1945 speech
There is no known force that can turn
an apple into an alley cat

pieces of the infamous rocket
once mocked by the U.S. government

love poem from his wife, Marjorie
Mine eyes are terrible
and strange, but
thou knowest me

recording of L. Ron Hubbard,
pre- his days with Scientology,
discussing with Jack
free love
and magic rituals

vials of dog blood

biography of an Earth Goddess

apology postcard from Marjorie
and Hubbard,
sent from some small island
off the coast of Spain—
It's better this way

sharpened swords to inspire
fear among his followers,
because freedom is a sword
with too many edges

photo of his Pasadena backyard
with Nobel Prize winners
posing among the lemon trees

half of his handsome face,
one hand clutching at his heart

tattered ingredient list—
    melding chemicals, togas
    saturated in his blood,
    testicle of one Hubbard
—the perfected formula for love

Beasts

They eat fruit from our gardens
and chickens from our coops, watch us
from trees like we're peculiar things.

We hunt them down in masses,
calling it sport, environmentalism,
an ode to first humanity.

If they could, I think they'd tear skin
from our corpses and wear us like shawls.
When I see you cleaning your rifle,

I avoid the thought of you
peeling, stripping, slicing, stabbing,
licking your lips in anticipation.

How you might adorn a part of me
across your shoulders, and from the rest
pick which tender parts to feast.

If I Moved to
Truth or Consequences

> Truth or Consequences, *the radio show, challenged the U.S. to rename a town in its honor. Hot Springs, New Mexico, officially changed its name.*
>
> *March 31, 1950*

I learned about it long after it's too late to talk city council
out of such a cheap publicity stunt,

but then I wonder if it wasn't, after all these years,
the perfect place to resolve myself.

Here I could be the woman who follows
assembly instructions, bends easily during yoga,

gets weekly massages, adopts a dog. Here, people
would subscribe to my allures and newfound serenity.

But even in this fantasy, I am quick to abandon everyone—
leave behind a dog who doesn't appreciate me,

a rented room that should've included cable,
all my possessions (which truthfully would only be

a throw I'd pretended to knit, and a self-portrait drunkenly
painted in a Sips 'n' Strokes class)—

making friends wonder what came of me, enduring so that I might become myth to Truth.

Or Consequence.

What I Meant
When I Said Love

life can only mean voice
only flesh
a polished surface
      always wanting

like how I wanted your hands
to be snakes
      down my shirt
poisonous temptation on skin

when you are gone
the air is warm and sick and
      just for one day
           still

Bless the Chocolate with Sprinkles

The day Dad said you didn't love us anymore,
I laughed, hard enough to bend in cramps.
By the time I realized it wasn't a joke,
my laughter was a thing
I could no longer control.
I ran away, or rather, quickly walked,
the rain a blessing
on my hot face.

I'd lost you once before,
in a crowded arcade.
I ran through each room
of headache-ripe colors
and pulsing noise, searching for
your easy, bright curls.
I grabbed your hand in relief
near the Skee-Ball,
pulled away, mortified,
when a stranger looked down.

At 13, I was shoeless and
only made it five blocks.
When he caught up,
I thought Dad would keep yelling,
but instead, he cried and I said nothing.
We both waited for him to be done.
Then, he set me in the car soaking wet,
and we went for ice cream.

Bless my father for breaking down,
me sick at the sight.
Bless the server scooping our cones,
> who pretended not to notice my wet socks
> puddling the tiled floor.

Bless the rain for making it too cold for ice cream,
the chocolate that froze my fingers,
> how I let it drip anyway.

Body Worship Takes Work

and years
and sometimes
forgiveness
it takes bribery
and solitude
and hands indebted
to breasts
it takes fingers
that mean *exist*
cascading to
an ass
that feels finally
like a pact
like sustenance
like coming
to terms with how
wrong you've been
it takes loving
those marks
sketched across
your inner thigh
because they show
growth because
beauty doesn't
mean sacrifice

beauty can be
finding out
your god is all hips
that her belly
is not
an apology.

Fish Love

1.
The first boy to touch me
threw me on a bed
and smothered my mouth
in his. It was garlicky
from the pizza
we'd just shared,
and I could tell this moment
was his, not mine,
so before I got too sad,
I became a fish—
quick, flexible, powerful
against any current,
yet easily caught.

I thought this was how
to be a woman in love,
which is to say I spent years
opening my throat for
man after man to gut.

2.
The story goes
that a rabbi finds a man
gutting fish by the river.
Why do you kill this fish?
the rabbi asks,
and the man replies,
Because I love fish.

How often is love nothing
more than fish love,
which is to say people
devour what it is
they love in you.

    3.
We met online,
which is to say we were doomed,
and yet you kept calling,
and I kept answering, and you kept
asking what it was you could give me,
and I didn't understand your kindness,
so I kept talking about fish.

I spoke of fish who can live
out of water for years.
Of fish who fling themselves
across land, using their fins to fly.
How fish moan and gnash
their teeth to talk.
How they hear through
reverberations
against their flesh,
which is to say
their tiny bones shudder
when something's coming.

But you saw through
my choreographed sidetracks;
you persisted, deeply human in
your devotion

… which is to say I'm out of my depths here.
Your warm words wash over me,
wash away my scales, fins,
the operculum and lateral line.
You are warming up my blood, again.

My love.
This poem is all just to say
I am finally listening.
And in hearing you,
I am resurrected,
fish no more.

About the Author

Bryanna Licciardi resists the question, "Where are you from?" She has lived all over the country—California, Texas, Michigan, Massachusetts, Louisiana—and currently resides in a small town near Nashville, Tennessee. She is a degree collector of sorts, with a BA from Austin Peay State University, an MFA from Emerson College, and a doctorate from Middle Tennessee State University. She works as an English lecturer and professional development coordinator, also at MTSU. Her spare time is spent taking care of four cats and one husband. Licciardi's first book, *Skin Splitting*, is a poetry chapbook from Finishing Line Press (2017). Her literary works have also appeared in such publications as *BlazeVox*, *Cleaver Magazine*, *Poetry Quarterly*, *Red Flag Poetry*, and *The Adirondack Review*. For more about her work, go to bryannalicciardi.com.

Endnotes

"Catch" features a definition from "A Glossary Guide to Swim Terms," *Fitter & Faster*, fitterandfaster.com/fun-and-games/glossary-guide-swim-terms, accessed April 11, 2022

"A Guilt Trap Has Many Teeth" borrows its title from a line by Stephen King.

Acknowledgments

"Double Dream" was originally published in *Strangelet Journal*

"Assigned Buddies" was originally published in *Rogue Agent Journal*

"Someone Sets Me Up with Charles Manson," "Eating Mercy," and "Interview with Mercy" were originally published in *Fourth & Sycamore*

"Hopalong Cassidy Was Grandmother's Hero" was originally published in *True Chili* and was featured in the short film *Quitting*

"Their Destroyed Mouths" was originally published in *Rockvale Review*

"Seasonal" was originally published in *The Underground Literary Journal*

"Temple Building" and "Twenty-Seven-Year-Old Virgin Sex Addict" were originally published in *BlazeVox 2kX*

"I'm 13 & Mom Convinces Me Period Blood Is Sacred" was originally published in *Wicked Banshee Press*

"Reimagining My Birth as Zeus & Athena" was originally published in *Dual Coast Magazine*

"Dealing" was originally published in *Abyss & Apex*

"Lies I Told My Baby Brother" and "Fragments of a False Elegy" were originally published in *The Indie Folk Music Review*

"Tidal Waves" was originally published as a postcard art project through *Red Flag Poetry*

"Trying to Reason with the Baby I Never Plan to Have" was originally published in *Crooked Teeth Literary Magazine* and republished in *Skin Splitting*

"Losing Weight" was originally published in *The Adirondack Review* and republished in *Skin Splitting*

"Thoughts I Don't Share While Out to Dinner with a New Guy" and "A Millennial's Unfinished Odes to Her Many Terrible Jobs" were originally published in *Poetry: A Wild Word Anthology*

"When the Bank Says My Account Was Drained" was originally published in *Pub House Books*

"20th Anniversary" was originally published as a feature in *Mud Season Review*

"H. H. Holmes Steals a Cadaver for Our Date" was originally published in *Dying Dahlia Review* as the poetry two-line contest winner

"A Guilt Trap Has Many Teeth" and "Reckoning" were originally published in *The Heartland Review*

"Mantras of an Anxious Child" and "If I Moved to Truth or Consequences" were originally published in *Peacock Journal*

"My Brother Tells Us about Catching Teenagers Stealing Shoes at the Department Store" was the first-place contest winner in *Floodmark*'s White Elephant Poetry Contest

"Dream Where My Teeth Fall Out" was originally published in *Northern New England Review*

"Found on or Near Jack Parsons' Body, Post-Blast" was originally published in *Spectral Lines: Poems about Scientists*

"Beasts" was originally published in *Skin Splitting* and was featured in teasers for the short film *Snapped*

"Body Worship Takes Work" was originally published in *Rascal Journal*

"Fish Love" was originally published in *The Mantle* and was nominated for a Pushcart Prize and a Bettering American Poetry Award

Author Thanks

A special thanks to my writing tribe, Chelsea Celestain and Kory Wells, for your gracious time and talent in helping me shape this book. Thanks to the poets Amy Wright, Amie Whittemore, and Gary McDowell for writing such kind things in support of this book. And finally, thanks to the team at Alternating Current for their fervent proofreading skills and cover art that perfectly captures this book's essence.

Colophon

The edition you are holding is the First Edition of this publication.

The title font is set in Adibafih, created by StringLabs. The secondary title font and page numbers are set in Avenir Book, created by Adrian Frutiger in collaboration with Monotype Type Director Akira Kobayashi. The Alternating Current Press logo is set in Portmanteau, created by JLH Fonts. All other text is set in Iowan Old Style, created by John Downer. All fonts used with permission and full commercial license; all rights reserved.

Cover jacket designed by Leah Angstman, with artwork by Wolfgang Eckert. The Alternating Current lightbulb logo was created by Leah Angstman, © 2013, 2024 Alternating Current. The interior fish were painted by artists at WatercolorPng. The fish divider was created by OpenClipArt-Vector. Some artwork is governed under a Pixabay Content License. Author photo by Kelly Chapman Photography. All images used with permission and full commercial license; all rights reserved.

Other Works from
Alternating Current Press

All of these books (and more) are available at
Alternating Current's website: altcurrentpress.com.

altcurrentpress.com